Tears and Forgiveness

Poems by

Amber Hardnett

978-0-578-77187-8

Dear Readers,

These poems that you are about to read are stories about a girl who has been lost for so long and is trying to find her way back to herself and her happiness. These poems are stories of how I still struggle everyday to be comfortable in my own skin, and how I fight for my happiness. I hope as you read my story it helps you in whatever you're facing. I pray that you find your peace and closure. I want you to know that you're not alone in this battle you're fighting. My story is for you to know that you will always have a friend in me. I want you to know that the darkest times don't last forever. The light inside you will shine again, and this time brighter than ever.

So to the readers, I want you to know that it's okay to cry, it's okay to not be okay. For the longest time, I would hide my tears because I thought it made me look weak, but sometimes you have to let it out in order to get better. Never let anyone tell you that your feelings don't matter, never ever anyone take away your happiness.

Acknowledgements

To myself: Thank you for showing me that no matter what life throws at me, I will always make it through the darkness. Thank you for being there for me whenever I didn't have anyone. To you, I want to say you are a fighter and a survivor. You deserve to be happy, loved, and free from all the pain.

To my granny and uncles: Thank you for all your love and support. Thank you for traveling 10+ hours to come visit me at school. Thank you for always putting up with my mood swings, and for always showing me love whenever I pushed you away.

To my sister: Thank you for always being by my side. Thank you for showing me that we are more than what we were faced with. Also, I want to thank you for being my number one supporter, and for pushing me to become a better version of myself. I will forever be your number one cheerleader, and promise to never let you settle for anything less than what you deserve. You are a fighter and I love you.

To Gina: I am beyond grateful to have you as my cousin. You have been there for me even when I would call thirty times in a row. Thank you for being my personal therapist, listening to me complains about failed relationship, and for being my person. Love you, Gina.

To Mrs. Tanya: From the bottom of my heart, I want to say that I'm forever grateful to have had you as my teacher, coach, and my English editor. Thank you for editing my papers, despite the fact that I usually waited until the last minute to ask. Words can't explain how grateful I am for all your help throughout these last few years.

To my friends: Thank you for pushing me out of my comfort zone, and always standing by me even when I push you away. Thank you for always being patient with me and my complicated feelings.

To my supporters: Thank you for reading this, supporting me, and believing in me. I want you to know that you are fighter, and you are never alone. You will always have a friend in me, and a shoulder to cry on.

Contents

Tears

Amber Hardnett

Tears on My Melanin Skin

As you roll down my face to release the emotions

I do not want to face

One by one you each tell a unique story

A story of unworthiness and guilt

A story of shamefulness and injustice

These tears on my melanin skin are a rush of hundreds of emotional stories

in one drop

I hate to see these tears on my melanin skin

You make me feel weakness

You make me feel angry

You make me feel empty

Tears why do you make me feel so weak and helpless inside?

These tears I shed when I'm alone

Alone to feel self- hate

Alone to think of all these negative thoughts

You want to feel all the scares and pain I refuse to face

All these tears on my melanin skin, and I can't stop them from falling

So tonight as I lay here and think about all the pain, self-hate, and guilt

I will let all these tears fall on my melanin skin

The stroke of her fingertips

As she put her fingertips on her keyboard
Her eyes quickly filled with tears
Tears from all the pain has carried over the years
As she types out her story on that old laptop she is afraid of seeing
Who she would be without the weight of pain she carried for years

For years the pain was part of her life, part of her personality
Part of how she loved and trusted people in her life
So as she types theses words, she asked herself if letting go of the pain
is really worth it?
She wonders if she would feel lost without the pain she carried
Her pain was her safety blanket for years
She wonders if people would truly love her for her, or
Would they want the pain to stay with so her personality wouldn't change?

Amber Hardnett

Thinking of you makes her hurt in ways she can't explain
Her eyes floods with tears, and she tries to turn them off
But the thought of you is just too strong for her will

I'm Not Okay

Feelings are very scary because you have to allow yourself to be completely vulnerable

Allowing myself to be completely open with myself scares the hell out of me

I have to keep reminding myself that it is okay to not be okay

The truth is that I am terrified of knowing the real me

Every day I face a constant battle with my inner self

I have to fight to get help because if not the pain wins

I fight to be happy so I won't cry any more painful tears

So these feelings I try to hide must now make their way to the surface

Time after time

You made your way onto her body everyday

Night fall and tears sets in her eyes

As he pressed his lips on her face her body got chills

The smell of you burned her stomach

She wants to scream for help but when she opens her mouth

Nothing ever comes out

Reflection

When she looks at herself in the mirror

She sees all the pain in her eyes that you left behind

From the one she loved the most

She prays that one day that all the tears you left will no longer be from pain

But for the happiness she will find

Burning Heart

You try to show her love, but all she felt was the pain

Her heart burned for your love

But all you kept giving her was disappointment

Heart, why don't you fill yourself with happiness

No more tears to fill the burning heart

She left you with

Tears and Forgiveness

She writes these words to you in hoping that will stop the flood

Of tears from falling on her face

As she sits in this dark room

You came in and wrecked her world

He slowly unzips his pants only to force her mouth on his penis

After that night her life changed forever

She tries to erase the memories of you

The scars on her body will never heal if the thought of you breaks her every time

She tries to hide the tears that rolls down her face

So that the world can't see how broken she is, and all the scars you left on her body

Suffocated by the tears you left on her skin

Come take back your tears

So I can breathe again

But once you get back your tears

She has a no return policy

So you can no longer suffocate her with the tears you left her with

The anger sits at the pit of her stomach
Itching to punch anything to remove the rage
Slowly feeling her body heat raising
Control breathing
Count to ten, but her body just infuses in rage
She tries to calm her inner voice
But the anger has reached her hands
Swinging to the sound of you voice fueled her anger

Mentally fucked up, but desperately wanting love

The two can't live in a world successfully

She screams for love, but she sprints the opposite direction when love is knocking on her heart

Past trauma left her emotionally damaged

Her loving you is like trying to win a game of tug-of-war in quick sand

It feels impossible for her to love when she is stuck in a game of tug-of-war with quick sand

Loving you would be easy if she wasn't emotionally damaged

Emotions of crying

Rush of water fills her eyes like tide hitting the shore

She so desperately wants it to stop

But the current of the tide is to strong

Waves after waves

Her body is in a tuga war with the waves that fills her brown eyes

These are waves of emotions that are followed by the rainfall of the tide

They fall one by one until the tide is completed

One o'clock

She is screaming for the tide to end

But the current is too loud to hear her scream

Amber Hardnett

Depression

Amber Hardnett

Depression is a thing I will never understand

One second you're happy and the next second you're in this mood that you really can't explain

You try so hard to fight it

But in the end, depression always wins

One day I will be able to look myself in the mirror and say I finally beat

This disease that took so much of my emotions

Depression, you will lose because my happiness will resurface again

Depression, you will not last forever

Trigger Warning

As she sits in this dark room, staring at the ceiling

You come into her bed just to show her your power, and while doing so

you wrecked her entire world

He slowly unzipped his pants, forcing your mouth on his penis

After that night her life changed forever

He robbed her of the innocence she could never get back

Amber Hardnett

Mother

I searched for her love, but all she ever gave me was heartbreak

I pray that one day she gives me the love that I missed out on for so long

I try to push the memories of you away so I will no longer feel the pain of your absent

All I wanted from you was to hear you say three simple words:

"I Believe You"

But instead you sided with the abuser, and for that you lost your oldest daughter

Your pride kept you from loving me whenever I needed you the most

Wondering Thoughts

Mind wondering as the nights grows shorter, and days get longer

These negative thoughts creeps up with no warning

She starts questioning her worth, wondering if she will ever be enough, wondering if she will ever learn how to love herself

These walls are starting to close in on her

As her mind begin to wanders faster

She's breathing heavily because these thoughts of not being loved or happy are a weight on her chest

She wants to break down those walls she has built over the years

Walls of vulnerability

Walls of fear

Walls of never trusting herself

Walls of never being happy

She wonders if anyone will come and help her break down these walls she has kept up for so long, or will they just show her why she had them from the beginning

You are a drug she can't fight

She pushes you to back of her mind hoping you will go away

But you somehow always seem to make your presence

She takes the twelve steps to recovery, but she just can't seem to get by step eight

By the end of her recovery she will able to say that she beat the drug that almost killed her

Tears and Forgiveness

Thinking of you makes her head aches and her eyes burn

You have brought nothing but pain into her life, and

All she wants to is to call out to you in her darkest night to feed her addiction of the pain you

left

The pain you left in her heart has overstayed its welcome

No- it's time for you to go harass another victim with your drug

It's time that her scars healed and her peace of mind restored

Amber Hardnett

You were the one thing that saves her in her darkest moments

You were there for her whenever she felt like the world neglected her

You came in the many sounds: sounds of pain, sounds of happiness,
and sounds of confusions

You gave her the peace whenever the world around her was chaos

So to you music she owes you everything and more

The sound of you kept her heart beating when pain almost killed her

Fight with Death

Death looks her in the eyes

She tries to run from him but her legs won't move

She asked him, why her? Why now?

Death replied because you refused to face the pain of letting go to heal your scars

From the ones that betrayed you

Her time is coming to an end unless she changes her state of mind, and lets go

of that drug that is killing her quickly

Don't let the spark die

Keep fighting for your happiness, the pain won't last forever

Peace will rise again

Happiness you will find her body and these tears won't fall again

Happiness she ask you not to take your time coming to her body

Friday After Next

Surrounded by these four brick walls

Laying down on your twin size bed

While you have your way with me

How could I say no whenever you were already inside me

<u>Friday After Next</u> playing in the background, and all I wanted was it to be over with

You weren't the first to have your way with me,

But you were the last one I let use for your own pleasure

He might say I wanted it, but how could he know since he never asked

We were just supposed to watch movies

But instead you made my night one to remember because my mind won't let me forget it

Tears and Forgiveness

11:59 my head is throbbing as I lay in bed thinking, and wondering why people always write me off before truly getting to know me.

Why do I always end up looking like a fool for trying to have a friendship or a relationship with people that clearly don't deserve me time?

It's now 12:03 and I can't sleep because the disconnect, the abandonment, and the thought of people is keeping me up at night.

I try so hard to block out the chaos, but I can't help to think of you because you were the root of all this chaos in my life.

But I know this chaos won't last forever.

I have to walk around acting like the chaos doesn't bother me, but deep down it's tearing me apart.

I wish you knew how you made me feel, so you would change your ways so you can stop hurting me.

To the people that hurt me in the past

Fuck you for making feel like there was something wrong with me; it's you that needs to re-evaluate yourself.

Amber Hardnett

A Year Later

October 19, marks a year you have been gone.

A year later without your laughter.

A year later without seeing your face.

A year later and I still can't wrap my head around the fact that you're gone.

There is not a day that goes by that I don't think about you.

There's so many things I wish I have done with you, and so many things I wanted to tell you.

A year later and the pain of not having you are still unbearable.

I know you're in a much better place now, and that you are no longer feeling pain.

But I wish I could just get one more day with you.

I love and miss you every day.

Rest peaceful and until we meet again, keep watching over me.

The dreams that came in a nightmare

Are these dreams or nightmares

All the pain and torture

Her body breaks out in sweats

Her mouth is full of blood from the pain she suffered

She is stuck in this sound proof room screaming to the top of her lungs

Just hoping someone will come and save her

She doesn't understand why these nightmares keep happening

She struggles to open her eyes from the nightmare she is running from

A moment goes by

Snap

The snapping of one's fingers brought her out of the nightmare

She kept reliving night after night

Her eyes finally open

But her mouth still has the taste of blood

So she wonders if part of her nightmare was real

Amber Hardnett

Never enough

Tossing and turning

The thoughts of never being enough runs through her mind

Wondering will today be the day

Flipping through her phone in and out of different apps

But nothing is getting that though out of her mind

She's trying to disconnect

But the thought grows stronger as she lays in silence

Still wondering if today is the day

Will this be the day they everyone in her life leaves her like that one that birth her?

Or

Will they surprise her and stay?

As she forces her eyes shut

Wishing sleep would hurry to find her

Only to wake to that today was not the day

Chaos of her thoughts

She is trying so desperately to breathe, but the chaos of her

thoughts were suffocating her

She is screaming for help, but no one hears her

Crying for the pain to stop

With sadness in her eyes, but still no one sees her

The world around her moving at the speed of light

Invisible to other by the burden of her pain

Fighting to stay alive

Day by day

But the chaos of her thoughts grows stronger

The war of depression finally came to an end

So when will be the right time to say her final goodbyes?

So she writes.....

To her love ones

Goodbye, sorry that it ended this way, but she couldn't take the pain anymore

As she takes her final breath with tears falling down her face

Knowing that this will be the last time you see her on this earth

Amber Hardnett

Preparing myself for the day you leave

One less call to lessen the pain

One less pointless conversation just to hear your voice

But all I want is the one last call

Not been able to see you will never get easier

The laughter we shared and the bond we had

Nothing will replace the love I carry for you

Sleep just a little longer

Cry a little harder

Scream a little louder

But nothing will ever bring you back to me

Why didn't you take me with you?

Why did you leave me so soon?

Can we just have one more day?

Twenty four hours, one thousand four hundred and forty four minutes is all I ask

The Screaming of the Tears

Sitting in the base of her eyes waiting until her body lets go of her pain

The tears are starting to take over vision, but the power of her body silence the rainfall

The tears are screaming to get out

Just let us go

You will be okay

You don't have to hold on to us anymore

Our time is up, and you got to heal

But her body continues to hold on, as the tears forces their way down her face

Her vision is clear, but her pain still lingers

As the screaming of her tears fall

Amber Hardnett

Searching for the words to express to you how I feel, but I can never seem to find the right
words

The scars you left me won't heal

My mind replays the images over and over

I distance myself from them, but the nightmares is still there

They all took a piece of me whenever they used me for their own pressure

But trying to forget is doing more harm than good

Dying inside over blurry images my brain keeps on a loop

Fighting a battle that feels impossible to win

But I'm still searching for the words because they never understand how I feel

Tears and Forgiveness

The names of my abusers flood my head

Cutting my tongue as their names leave my mouth

One by one I release the pain you left me with

I disguised your name to protect your face

But I release the details of your body

The blood that connected us

Brown skin, tall, males

These are the similarities you shared as you used me for your own pleasure

Average height

Shoulder length hair

With the same characteristics of me

While using me for your own pleasure

You all left traumatized memories

Afraid to sleep because seeing your face and saying your name has left my tongue raw

Amber Hardnett

Love

Amber Hardnett

A Kiss

A kiss in time we shared as one regret

You kissed me one drunken night

The kissed that hunt the one you like

Unanswered questions is to why the kiss, but in the end the kiss was one drunken night

Friends we may never be for something that is simple as a little kiss

One fights for the friendship that may never by

While you always be a friend to me

Truth is told you kissed me, but in the end it was just on drunken night

A drunken night with unanswered questions

This caused a strain on a friendship that one regretted

For one drunken kiss that never should have happened

Ex-Friends

To the end of a friendship of unknown

We may never know what cause this strain

To you I'm sorry for this pain

Ex friends we will never be

Distance in time that will heal your pain

For we will never be ex friends

We laugh we shared but in the end the pain was too much

But I just want you to know we will never be ex friends

I hope you find your peace

Cheers to the end of a friendship that was never completed

Ex-friends we will never be

Amber Hardnett

The thought of you gives me butterflies

You calm me even when you don't realize it

You give me hope that I could find love in the chaos world

I've fallen for your mind, and how you're always there for when I needed a friend to listen

Months after months you have gotten to know me more than anyone else

With you I felt completely safe

The thought of you makes my heart happier than it ever has been

Your face is a blur, but your mind is astonishing

Maybe this is just me falling to fast

But if I don't try then all this would be for nothing

I go to sleep at night wondering if I will ever see your face

But at the end of the day, you're just a notification on my phone

Tears and Forgiveness

2:04 am all that's on her mind is that she will never know what your love felt like

She wonders what she could have done differently to make you as more than a friend

She sees your notification pop up on her phone, but wonder if she should open it

All she wants is to kiss the lips that broke her heart

The love she has for you is a love she thought she would never feel again

Ding! Notification from you

Take a deep breath

Opens the notification and she show her worse nightmare come true

You with the one you love so now she has to say good bye

Goodbye California our time must end here so her heart can't break anymore

Amber Hardnett

Her love is rare

Her love is pure

But she can never find the one to share her love with

One day she hopes to love freely

But until then the love will be locked away

But hopes that her love won't be locked away forever

Will someone find the right key to unlock this rare love she pushed away to keep from getting
hurt

True love, self-love, and love itself are hard for her to feel

But maybe one day she will find the right key to help with self-love

But until then, she fills her heart with strong like the ones she cares the most about

Tears and Forgiveness

You are the one feeling she can't escape

People tell her to move on, but thought of losing you would kill her

You're the one drug she doesn't want to fight because that would mean she couldn't

have you anymore

Before she knew it, you consume her whole life

All she ever wanted was to wrap you in her arms one last time

Before you were completely gone from her mind

Your smell, your touch, your love

She will never know how any of this feels because you gave all that

and more to someone else

Amber Hardnett

Brown eyes long sandy brown hair
You were the one I could never call mine
Our world crashed after a kiss was shared
The kiss that forever changed my life

Deep down I always wanted for our lips to touch
But I didn't think I would lose in the process
Things begin to spiral and after that there was no going back

Your hugs were always my favorite because begin in your arms is where I felt the safest
March of 2018 was the last time I got to be in your arms
To this day, I wish I could stop time so I could have been with you for just a minute longer

But even though you were the one that got away
You will always have a home in my heart

Tears and Forgiveness

Since the girl of her dreams she thought she would never feel again

But then you came along

Part of her wished she never let it go that far

But looking at you as the light from the moon reflected off your skin made her want you more

She just has to say that she will ruin this before if even happens

Too many texts and calls

We should have just stayed friends now she is trapped because all she wants is to be next to you

So now she has no choice but to turn off her feelings for you

So she can spare herself from the disappointment

So please don't take it the wrong way when she distances herself from you

Amber Hardnett

Hearing you say my name makes me weak in the knees

Your lips pressed against my neck

Why did you do this to me?

Now how do I look at you and not want to put my hands all over you?

You did this to me and now how do you expect me to turn this off

I close my eyes, and I can still feel you

I feel your lips on my body

I feel your hand in my hand

I feel your fingers inside of me, and

watch you lick me off of you.

Tears and Forgiveness

Tonight I cut all ties to you

No more pointless conversation

Awkward stares from across the room

Tonight you made your choice and it wasn't me

I guess you're happy with that choice

Even though we both know you're better off without either of us.

You changed, the moment our lips touched each other

All I have to say to you is that congratulations for making feel like everyone else did

Not good enough and like something is wrong with my body

But you got your wish

I will delete you from my phone so I won't get the urge to text you

will keep your mistake a secret but I will not let you treat me like I did something wrong to you

The thought of you brings tears to my eyes
I can't tell if they are happy or sad tears
The bond we have made were only through an app

We both agreed in the beginning that this was just a friendship
But over time that slowly started to change to for me
You were there for me in ways I didn't allow people
To me you are my Cali Girl
Who I hope would one day feel the same way I feel about you

I go back and forth in my mind on wither or not if I should express my feelings
The thought of losing you right now break me
Even though I'm slowly losing you to another person
These feeling I have for you is driving me crazy because
We have only connected through an app
But to me you will always be my Cali Girl.

The taste of her is a mystery

As she lays here in her bed trying to find the right words to ask you a simple thing

She wants you, but not in that way

She wants her face to be buried deep between your thighs, and her fingers inside you

While she listens to the sound of you moaning

She wants to you say stop even though you want more

So how does she find the right words to say all this to you?

Three simple words, but she finds it so hard to send the message

She wants to taste your lips on her tongue for one night

But she never finds the right words to ask a simple question

She needs to feed her addiction of wanting to taste your lips

She asks for one night, but she knows if she gets one taste of your lips then she will want more than just that

She asks herself, what are the right words to send to you so she can taste you for one night?

I fought back my urge to text you a simple "hey" to avoid a dry conversation

I thought we were friends, but you changed the moment things got weird

I just want to know why you changed

But its best if I left things unsaid

I hate that I can't get you out of my head

You found me in my dreams

So now I have no place to go to escape from your face

But all I want is a simple answer as to why have you been treating me like shit?

What did I do that was so bad to make you do the things you did to me?

I just want you out of my dreams

The first day she has went without hearing your voice

Secretly hoping that your name will come across her screen

Trying her hardest not to text you, but she did anyway

Just wanting to hear your voice

Flipping back and forth through our messages

Because that is all she has left of you

You were the one rose she thought she could love in a field of sunflowers

But you had other planes that didn't involve her

But maybe, just maybe your name will come across her screen tomorrow

You are the only person she wants to share her day with

The person who she loves to share her poems with

Because lately you are all she can write about

You are the first and last thing she thinks about

Deprived of a body that her fingers never touched

Wanting to get you out of her head because you already got her out of yours

The image of you pops in her head leaving her blushing for an image she can't touch

Dreaming that your name popped up on her phone

Only to wake up to a dream

Coming to the realization that she came into your life at the wrong time

But not regretting the time they shared

You weren't ready to feel again

And she was ready to feel everything

Hoping they path cross again at the right time

But until then they keep their distance

She misses the touch of you pressing against her

The smell of you has slowly faded from her favorite hoodie

The sound of your voice no longer brings a smile to her face, but tears to her eyes

She fights the urge of texting your phone

She goes to delete your message thread, but hesitates because that's the last piece
she has left of you

You left because she couldn't find the words for you to stay

You left because trying was too hard

Her eyes filled with tears not because you left, but because she was starting to feel enough

But then you went to find happiness with another person

Loving you was never hard

I knew that you would never feel the same

That was the hard part

But evening knowing that

It never stopped me from falling for you

Reciprocation of love

How does she love when her love always failed her?

Her heart full of scars and all she wants is to be loved

Scars after scars

Heartbreak after heartbreak

She still search for love

In hope that one day her love is reciprocated

Mid morning phone call

Three o'clock in the morning
She jumps up out her sleep
For their routine phone call
She turns over to look at her phone
But she doesn't see a missed call from you

She stays up for a few more minutes
Hoping your call would come through
Three-twenty hit
She realizes that you are not calling

She rolls back over and falls asleep
With sadness in her eyes
The sound of your voice puts her heart at ease
But this morning she panicking
At fear of not knowing if you were safe

Maybe tonight she will receive your call
As she waits mid morning for that incoming call

Second Choice

I wanted to protect you from the world, but you weren't ready to let go

Still the best part of my day even though you're no longer here

The conversation we shared while carrying the hurt from you other people

We both wanted to be loved, but only one found love

I'm still second to the one that hurt you, blinded by the love in your past

while losing the love of your future

I wish you the best, but I hate being your second choice

Grabbed you by the neck as she kissing you

Whispering sweet nothing into your ears while she working her way down your body

Slowly spreading your thighs as the tension between you too build

Gliding her finger down your body into an ocean of your juice

Inserting herself inside you as she moans to the pleasuring of your fingers

Kissing on your thighs as she makes her way to your ocean

Flipping her over on her back while you ride her face to the sound of music

Amber Hardnett

Writing about you never gets old

Our love story will be one for the book

Finding a sunflower in a field of roses

I was your first choice, and you scream it to the world

A love like ours is end game

And you will always be my favorite sunflower

Best Part

She loves sending you good morning texts

You are the best part of her day

Hearing your voice is a sweet melody that makes her heart skips a beat

Slow dancing in the park to the music on her phone

Wishing the night will last forever

Because the best part of her was loving you

Even though her heart is in a million pieces

She still finds a way to love you

You tapped her heart back together only to break it again

Giving up would be easy, but her heart still beats for love

Dressed in disguise of a sunflower only to end up as a rose

Beautiful, innocent, soft, and yet filled with thorns

The token of love, but never feel love when you're around

Tears and Forgiveness

The image of you is stuck in my head

I lay up at night looking at your photos imaging that you were next to me

I want to bury myself between your thighs, while you say my name

I want to hold you inside my arms, and protect you from the world

I wanted to be the one that brings you happiness, instead of heartbreak

You're the breath of fresh air when I feel like the world is suffocating

Your beautiful hazel eyes is like a field of sunflowers

Looking into your eyes just makes my day ten times better

Your eyes bring me peace in the chaos of my thoughts

The sound of your voice is music to my ears

You're the best part of my day that I don't want to lose

Amber Hardnett

Dangerously wanting her body

Photos of her flashing through my mind like motion pictures

Every inch of her body beautifully captured as the sun radiate from her brown skin

Her luscious lips shinning from her lip gloss

Staring into her eyes is like standing in a field of sunflowers

Kissing my soul with her beautiful hazel eyes

Hopelessly pinning for your love

Only to have it taken away from a ghost in your past

Tears and Forgiveness

She keeps trying even though you are continuously pushing her away

The same conversation over and over

Push and pull

Push and pull

But how much more pushing will she take until you push her away for good?

You are scared of having feeling for someone who is willing to give you the world but who isn't

Love is scary but is also the best feeling ever

But she isn't asking for you to love her just asking for you to let her in

Distancing yourself isn't going to stop her from caring about you

She wants to be a shoulder for you to cry on

Someone who makes you smile when you're at your worst

She just wants to be enough for you because you're enough for her

So she asking you stop pushing her away, and just let her be a friend to you

Amber Hardnett

She had eyes of a goddess but the tongue of the devil

Her eyes gave you hope

When her tongue gave you lie

So which one do you trust?

When both sound like music to your ears

Fighting for a chance only to be pushed away

Stay

She pushed you away to see if you would leave

She was never your first choice

So leaving her was easy

She lay up at night crying because in the end

She never know what it feels like for someone to stay

Stay through her unexplained emotions

Stay through her trust issue

Stay through her silence

Stay for when she can't find words to tell you to stay

In the end she just wanted you to stay, but you chose to leave

Amber Hardnett

Forgiveness and Acceptances

Amber Hardnett

Forgiveness why won't you let her forget
Forgive her for the pain that she will never forget
Her mind plays over and over like a broken record
Forgiveness is the hardest part to her healing
Her heart is broken because of the pain she can't forget

Forgiveness why are you so hard on her
Tears in your eyes
Memories haunt her in the dark
She looks at you and forgiveness never comes
Her tears fall down her face because she knows that forgiveness will never come

She waits and waits but the forgetting of her pain will never let her forgive
The demons that stay in her head
Forgiveness, forgiveness why are you so hard on her
She closed her eyes to dream forgiveness
But all she gets is pain

The Tears Dried Out

The tears I cried for you no longer fall

On my beautiful brown skin

The anger I carried is no longer there

I don't know if I have forgiven you, but I am at peace

I've made my peace with this being the new normal

When I look at you, I see a mother who is trying

I see a better bound

The tears are dry and the pain is gone

But the memories are forever

Amber Hardnett

My sister keepers

I'm my sister keeper

I'm my sister protector

We've been through so much, and trauma

I will love you until my last breathe

I will forever be my sister keeper

She is always be my biggest cheerleader

She is funny, beautiful, smart, and have a heart of gold

I will always fights for her, because of her I've overcome several different obstacles

She is the reason I push myself to be the best woman, friend, and sister I can be

I'm my sister keeper

I pray that she gets everything she deserves, and find loves within herself

Our past took a lot of our childhood from us, but I will not let it take our future

I will forever be my sister keeper, and her protector

Our bond will never be broken

I'm my sister keeper, and she is my strength

The Unknown Sea

A place where your mind goes for clarity and peace

A place of the unknown sea

The sea of darkness and pain

The place of the unknown sea

You search and search for clarity and peace

But all you find is the place of the unknown sea

To find the answer of the unknown sea

You must restore what is broken

To find the answer of the unknown sea

Answers you may find to heal the scars from the loss of a friend

With closure you may never know

To find the answer of the unknown sea

Made in the USA
Columbia, SC
28 March 2021

35224047R00048